Equestrian Moments

Touching the Heart of a Horse

ii

Equestrian Moments

Touching the Heart of a Horse

Marc C. Ness

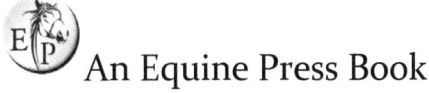

An Equine Press Book

Copyright © 2018 Marc C. Ness

All rights reserved. No part of this book may be reproduced or utilized in any form or by any means, electronic or mechanical, including photocopying, recording, or by any information storage and retrieval system, without permission in writing from the publisher.
The scanning, uploading, and distribution of this book via the Internet or any other means without the permission of the publisher are illegal and punishable by law. Your support of the publisher's rights is appreciated.

ISBN: 0692185682
ISBN 13: 978-0692185681

Without the unending generosity of a horse, this book would not be possible. Thank you for being a friend.

Introduction

The inner world.

For most equestrians, life around a horse is something they wouldn't consider as separate from their everyday lives. They don't think of the subject as something detached from everyday experience. To be close to their horse, to know its every movement, to feel its emotions and connect with it on a personal level, is far too intimate an experience to cast off as something outside of themselves. For them, the encounter can't be dissected like a corpse to identify the anatomy of an animal.

Their purpose is less about riding methods and theories than it is about an inner experience that eludes explanation. They strive to achieve something more profound than a typical gathering of information; they push themselves to comprehend what their horse perceives. Aiming to deepen their understanding, they look past manufactured results of an exterior nature and journey into the origins of the inner universe where personal experience reins king, and the heart sends its message one beat at a time.

Most, but not all equestrian theory tends not to extend beyond the intellect. It concentrates on the exterior world of facts, figures, and physical technique, showing a limited, incomplete view of the equestrian world. While this method has merits, the larger world of thoughts and emotions contains the deeper individual experience of genuine connection. It springs from the inner world, where intuitive impulses form the very fabric of personal perception.

Classifying all the horses in the world tells you little about the workings of a horse, and even less about the miraculous personal events that occur between horse and rider. Consequently, diagramming the most complex equestrian theories, in a similar fashion, divorces you from any real comprehension of a horse, or the broader perceptions of horse and human relationships.

The subjective feeling of our encounters with horses is an intimate, moment to moment experience of practical significance. Instinctive, spontaneous impressions rise to the surface of the mind revealing secrets of communication that cannot be understood intellectually alone. They require an emotional sensitivity to become whole. They live in the motion of our souls, in the wondrous activity of our hearts and minds.

When you sit in the saddle, centered and calm, even though you may have knowledge of the bodies anatomy; its addition will not increase your skill. In quite the same fashion, a professional rider of great talent and ability may have the instinctive sense of how to ride a horse while not knowing the first thing about anatomy. The child, riding a pony with exuberance across a hay meadow, understands in the deepest terms far more than a trainer who has on his tongue all the breeds of all the horses in the world.

Your body knows how to correct its balance in the saddle; a horse knows how to jump over an obstacle. This inherent miraculous knowledge is acted upon by the body, making all physical movement possible. Your emotional life finds a balance as well; it tends toward equilibrium. After strong emotional turmoil, it rests between the highs and lows of the swinging pendulum, bringing you to a peaceful place where deeper connections abound.

It is the direct, intimate encounter with another that forms the foundation of any relationship. The mysterious subjective connection between horse and human is the basis for improving your equestrian skills.

Think of your horse, dare to study the quality of its life, ignore the advice of others unless it steadfastly follows the nature of your own experience. Reflect on the essence of your understanding, ride the emotional mobility between horse and human and you will comprehend the very nature of the universe. More can be revealed to you by a horse in a single equestrian moment than the education of a lifetime.

As you read this book, look between the lines to those hidden realities that lovingly bring you to direct contact with your horse. Explore the intimate connection of the heart, where horse and human relationships fill your life with perceptible comprehensions of joy.

Marc C. Ness

Acknowledgment

Whatever your discipline, every equestrian can agree, few horses stand as paramount in our lives. For every one of us, it's the heartfelt connection of that one horse which fills our hearts with joy. In your own unique way, touch your horse with a caring hand and a loving heart. Without this vital experience, it would be just another game.

"Intimacy is the private atmosphere in which all things reveal the truth of themselves."

FALSE PRETENSE IS A MASK THAT HIDES THE REAL BEAUTY BENEATH, HAVE THE COURAGE TO SHOW YOUR TRUE SELF.

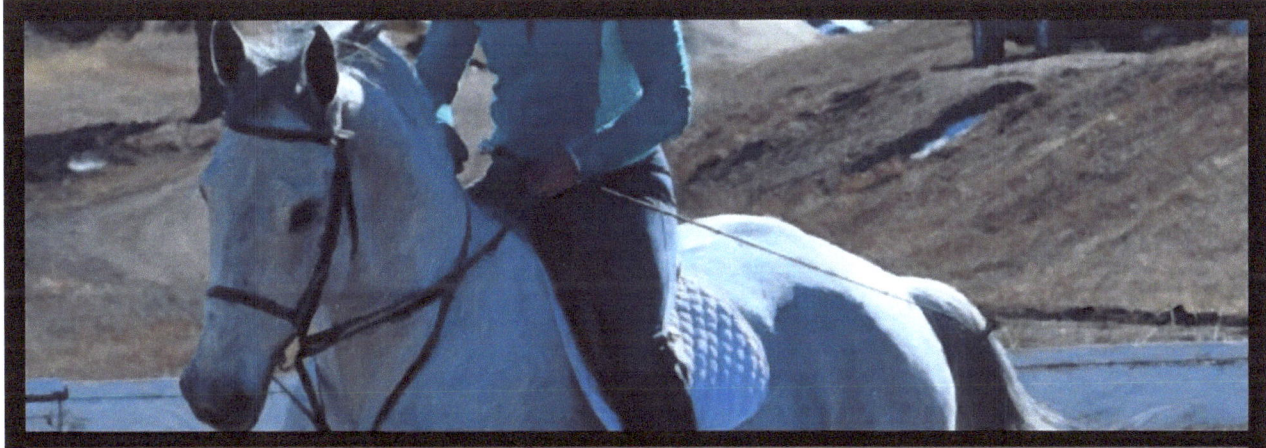

BEAUTY IS FOUND IN ACCEPTANCE; A HORSE WILL ACCEPT WHAT YOU OFFER. **BUT GIVING A FALSE PRESENTATION** OF WHO YOU ARE IS NOT SINCERE. SHOW YOUR TRUE **SELF, AND YOUR HORSE WILL RESPOND.**

BEAUTY IS FOUND IN ACCEPTANCE

THE ACCURACY OF YOUR DISCERNMENT REVEALS THE QUALITY OF YOUR TRUTH.

IS IT ACCURATE

THE VOID IS NOT EMPTY

WHAT IS THE CONCEPTION OF YOUR HORSE? IS IT ACCURATE, OR IS IT WHAT YOU WANT IT TO BE? FOR INTIMACY TO REVEAL ITSELF, THERE NEEDS TO BE ABANDON. THE VOID IS NOT EMPTY; IT CONTAINS REALITY, THE BEATING HEART OF A HORSE.

PEACE IS A STATE OF TRANQUILITY THAT DISSOLVES THE SEPARATION BETWEEN YOU AND THE WORLD.

YOU NEED PEACE

WHEN YOU RIDE YOUR HORSE ARE YOU PEACEFUL? MOST PEOPLE RIDE WITH A SENSE OF EXCITEMENT; THEY SIT WITH THE NERVOUS ENERGY OF THE EXPECTATION OF HAPPINESS. YOU NEED PEACE TO GAIN A CLOSENESS WITH YOUR HORSE; PEACE IS THE FOUNDATION OF TRUE INTIMACY.

PHYSICAL TOUCH CENTERS YOU IN EXPERIENCE, IT SAYS I AM HERE WITH YOU.

BE AWARE OF EVERY DETAIL

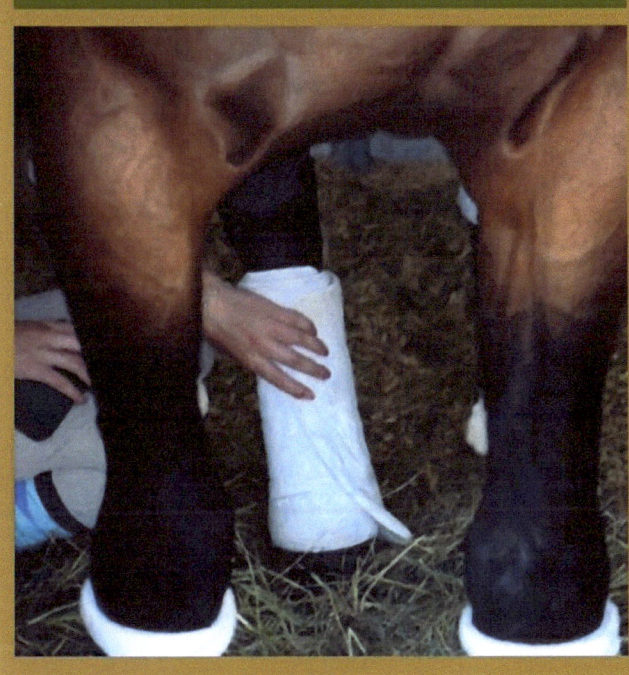

WHEN YOU ARE GROOMING YOUR HORSE STAY IN THE MOMENT, BE AWARE OF EVERY DETAIL IN YOUR CARE. INTIMACY IS AVAILABLE BY LETTING GO OF THE FUTURE. THAT IS THE WAY TO BUILD A RELATIONSHIP, ONE GENTLE TOUCH AT A TIME.

YOUR THOUGHTS FORM THE QUALITY OF YOUR DIRECTION, WATCH THEM CLOSELY.

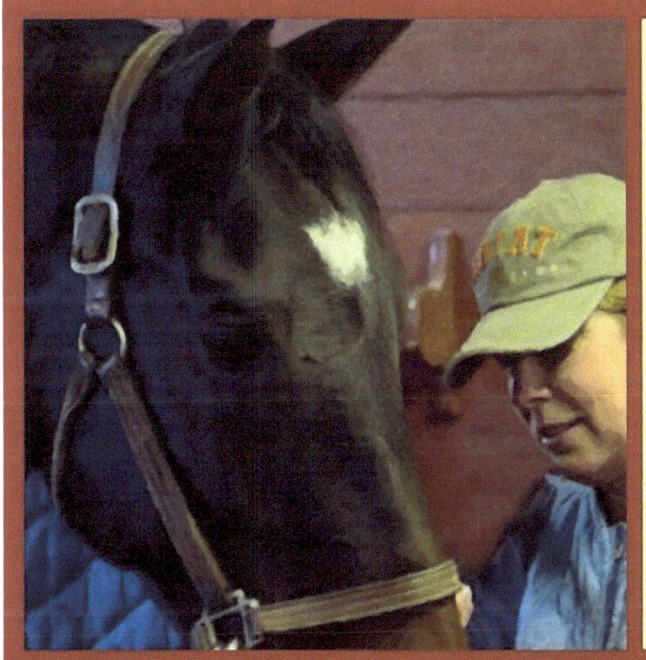

BE COOPERATIVE IN YOUR THOUGHTS

WHAT THOUGHTS DO YOU HAVE TOWARD YOUR HORSE? ARE THEY ARGUMENTATIVE, CONTROLLING? WHY DO YOU THINK HE DOESN'T WANT TO LISTEN? BE COOPERATIVE IN YOUR THOUGHTS AND ACTIONS; IT WILL GO A LONG WAY TOWARDS ACHIEVING WHAT YOU WANT.

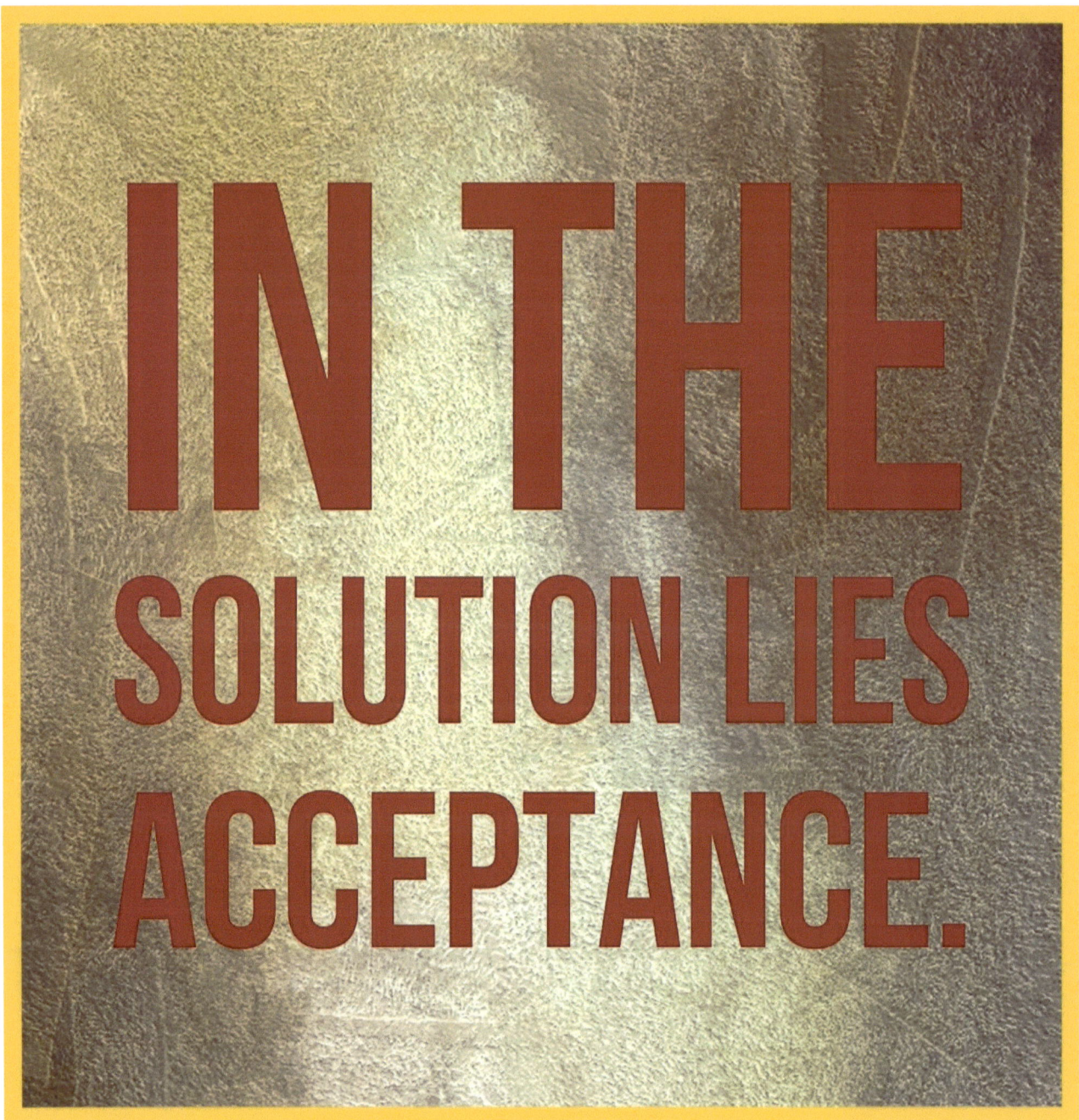

WHAT HORSE ARE YOU RIDING TODAY?

THE QUITE GENTLE ONE OR THE FIERY STALLION? WHATEVER THE STATE IS, ACCEPT IT. EMBRACE THE SITUATION WITH **COMPASSION AND UNDERSTANDING.** THIS TELLS YOUR HORSE YOU ARE ON HIS SIDE, YOU **KNOW WHAT HE FEELS, THEN YOU FIND A PARTNER** IN THE SADDLE, NOT AN ENEMY.

TRUST IN YOURSELF AND YOUR ABILITY TO CONNECT

KEEP AS FEW POSSESSIONS AS POSSIBLE, DON'T LET OLD IDEAS DICTATE YOUR RELATIONSHIP WITH YOUR HORSE. LET GO OF THE THOUGHTS THAT CREATE A DISTANCE IN YOUR FRIENDSHIP. TRUST IN YOURSELF AND YOUR ABILITY TO CONNECT.

KEEP AS FEW POSSESSIONS AS POSSIBLE

THE TRUTH IS SOMETIMES THE HARDEST THING TO HEAR.

Do you listen to your horse or do you expect her to listen only to you? **Communication** is a two-way street. If one side is more heavily weighted, an imbalance **occurs. Open** yourself to listening, even if it's not what **you want to** hear. True dialogue is the basis for any **relationship.**

HONEST INTROSPECTION CLEARS THE WAY FOR CLOSER RELATIONSHIPS.

TO FIND THE TRUTH

NOT TOWARDS SELF-DELUSION

DO YOU KNOW YOUR HORSE? DO YOU UNDERSTAND ITS NEEDS AND DESIRES? MOST OF US THINK WE DO, BUT AFTER A LITTLE INTROSPECTION, WE FIND THAT ISN'T TRUE. TO FIND THE TRUTH, WE MUST THROW AWAY OUR PRE-CONCEIVED IDEAS. INTIMACY IS FOUND BY MOVING CLOSER TO SOMETHING REAL, NOT TOWARDS SELF-DELUSION.

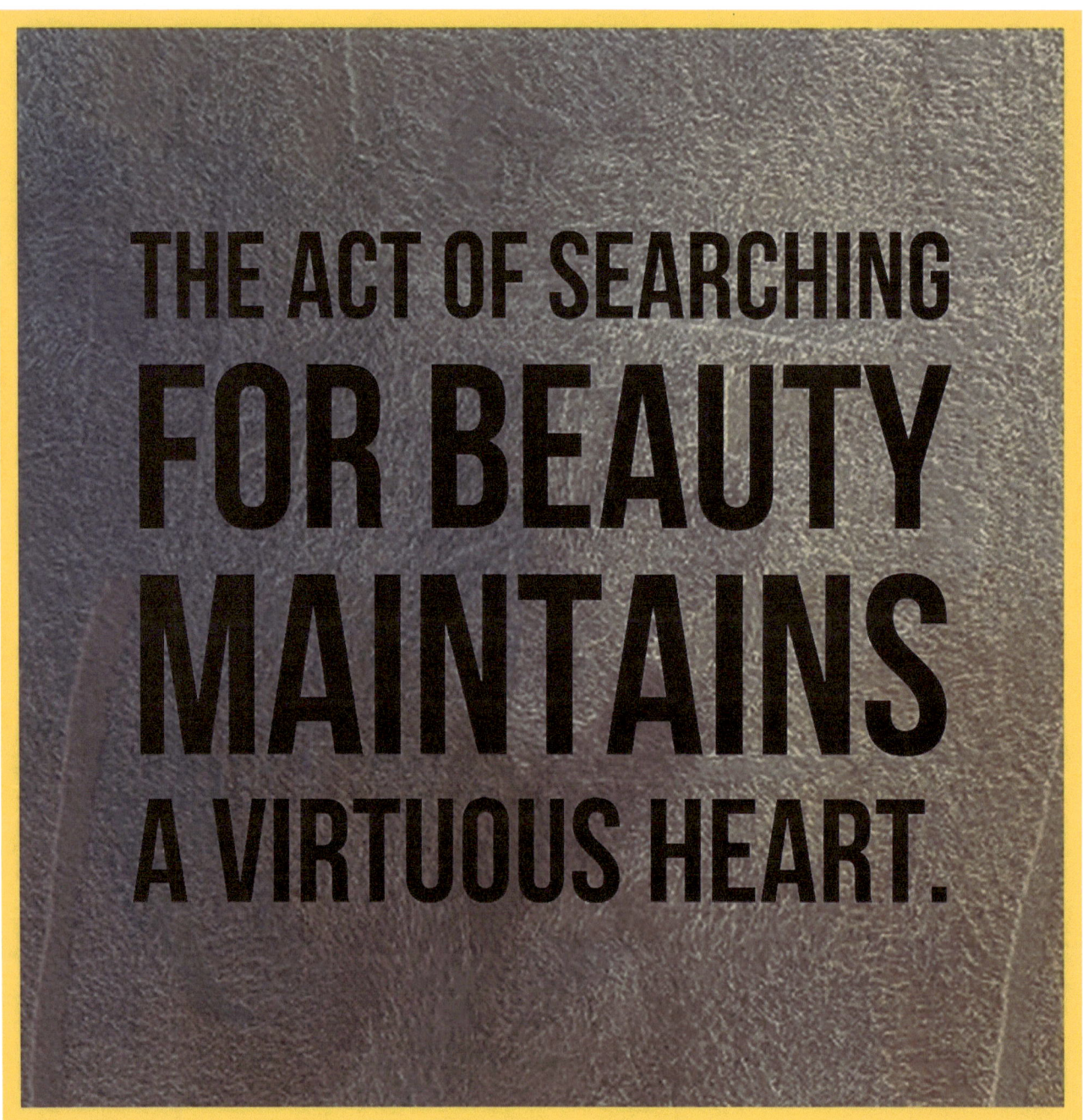

DROP THE BARRIERS IN YOUR MIND

INTIMACY STARTS WITH YOU, RIGHT HERE, IN THIS MOMENT. DROP THE BARRIERS IN YOUR MIND THAT KEEP YOU FROM PERCEIVING BEAUTY, THE ESSENCE OF YOUR HORSE—THE HEART.

LEARN TO APPRECIATE THE VALUE OF A POSITIVE ATTITUDE.

DO YOU KNOW WHAT A SADDLE BLANKET IS USED FOR? IT PROTECTS YOUR HORSE FROM IRRITATING MATERIAL BETWEEN ITSELF AND THE SADDLE. BUT PHYSICAL NATURE ISN'T THE ONLY THING TO GUARD AGAINST; THERE ARE NEGATIVE THOUGHTS THAT KEEP A RELATIONSHIP DISTANT. WEAR GRATITUDE LIKE A SADDLE BLANKET, IT BUFFERS TENDERNESS FROM CALLOUS IDEAS AND MAINTAINS A CONNECTION BETWEEN TWO SOULS.

WEAR GRATITUDE LIKE A SADDLE BLANKET

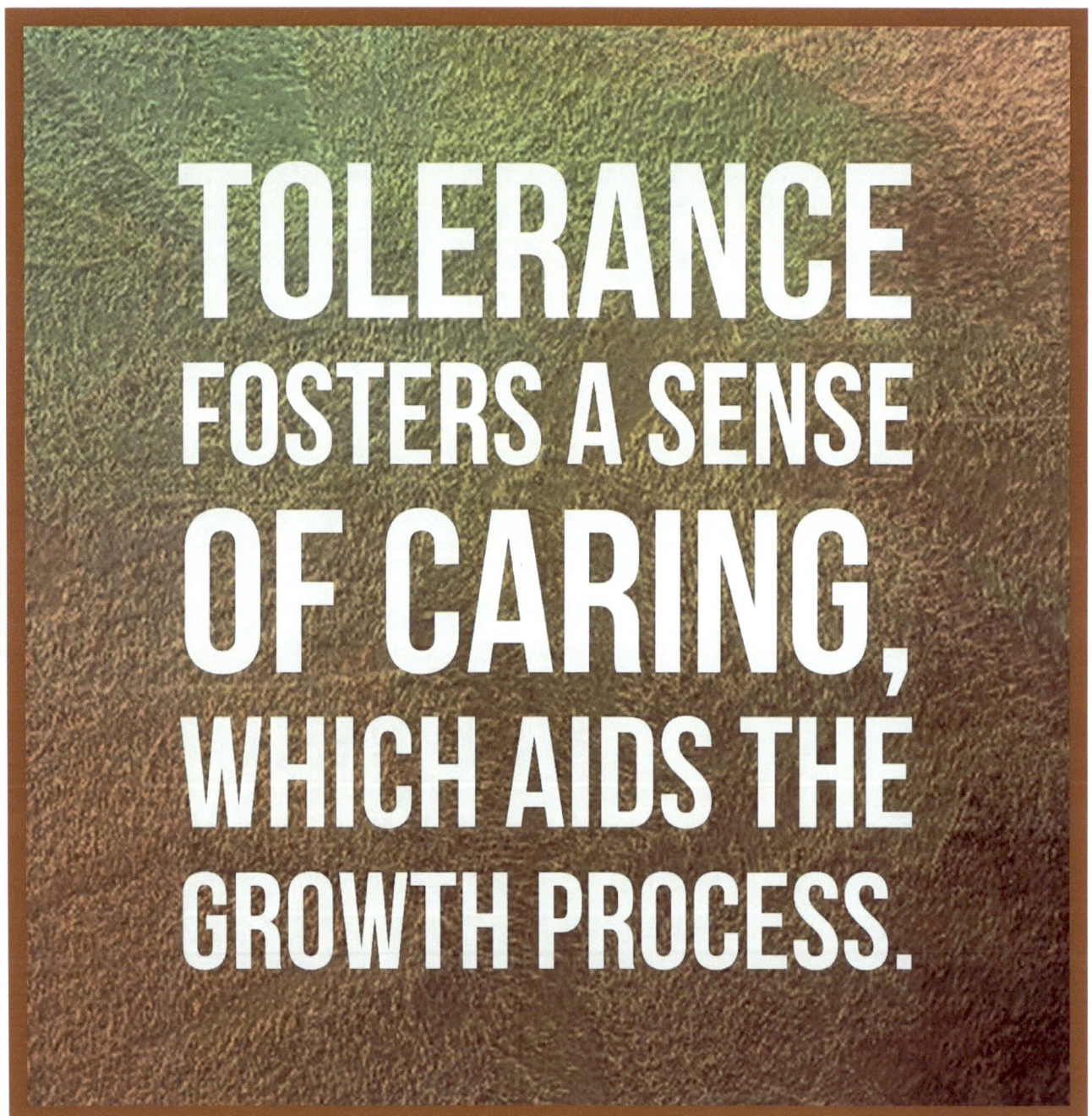

TOLERANCE FOSTERS A SENSE OF CARING, WHICH AIDS THE GROWTH PROCESS.

DAY AFTER DAY, YOUR HORSE LISTENS TO YOUR AIDS, DOING WHAT YOU ASK. WHEN YOU STRUGGLE TO TEACH A LESSON, HAVE A COMPASSIONATE HEART. LET IT KNOW, I AM WITH YOU, NOT AGAINST YOU. THEN IT WILL PERFORM MIRACLES.

I AM WITH YOU

HAVE A COMPASSIONATE HEART

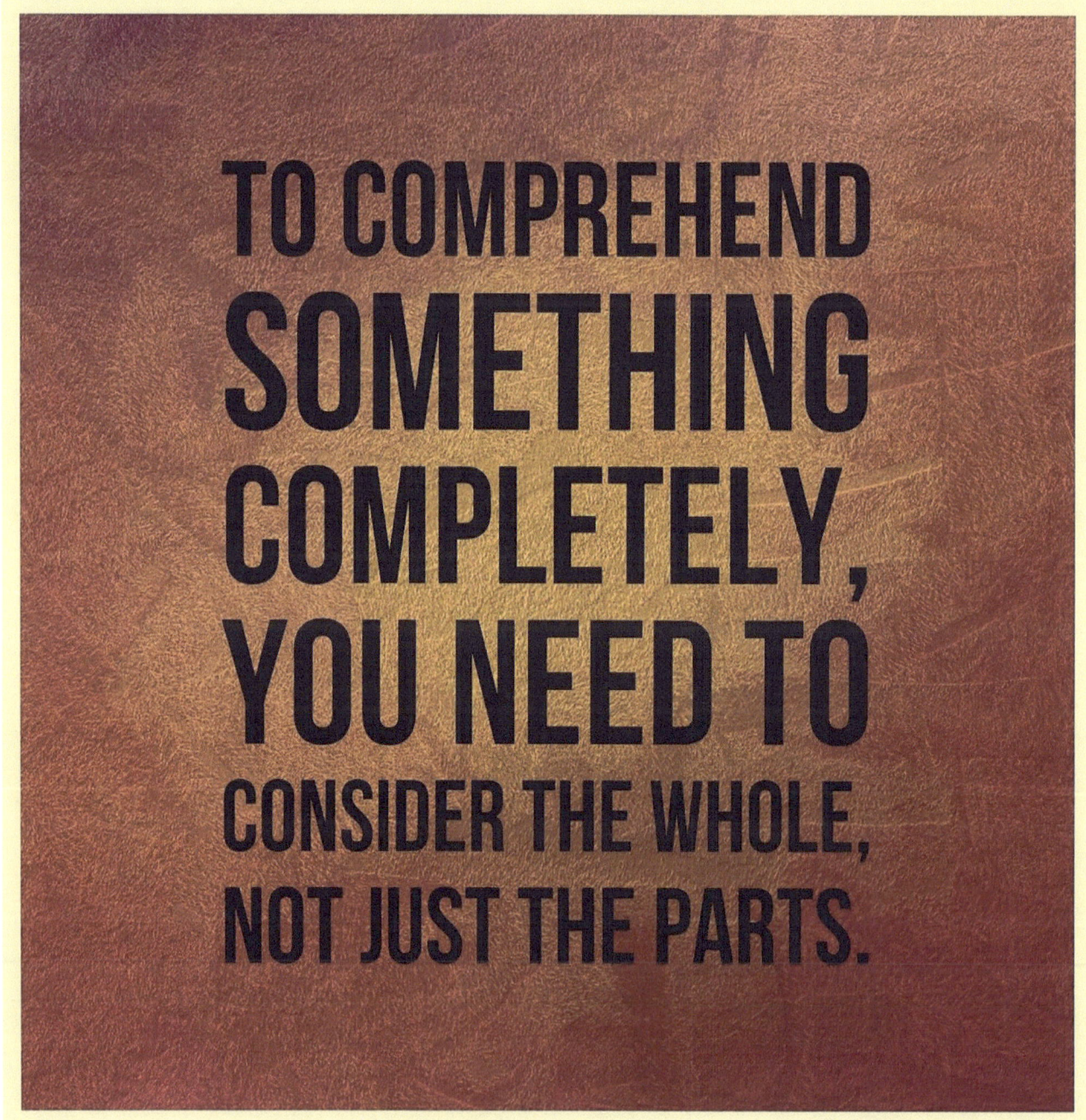

UNDERSTANDING REQUIRES EXPERIENCE

TO SIT AND WAIT FOR YOUR HORSE TO CHANGE, IS NOT AN ACT OF PATIENCE. TO HOPE THAT A NEGATIVE TRAIT WILL SOMEDAY WASH AWAY IS PURE NONSENSE. PATIENCE IS LOOKING AT THE WHOLE, CONSIDERING BOTH GOOD AND BAD QUALITIES. TRUE EQUESTRIANS KNOW THE YOUNG HORSE TAKES TIME TO MATURE, UNDERSTANDING REQUIRES EXPERIENCE **TO COMPLETE A TENDER HEART.**

PATIENCE IS LOOKING AT THE WHOLE

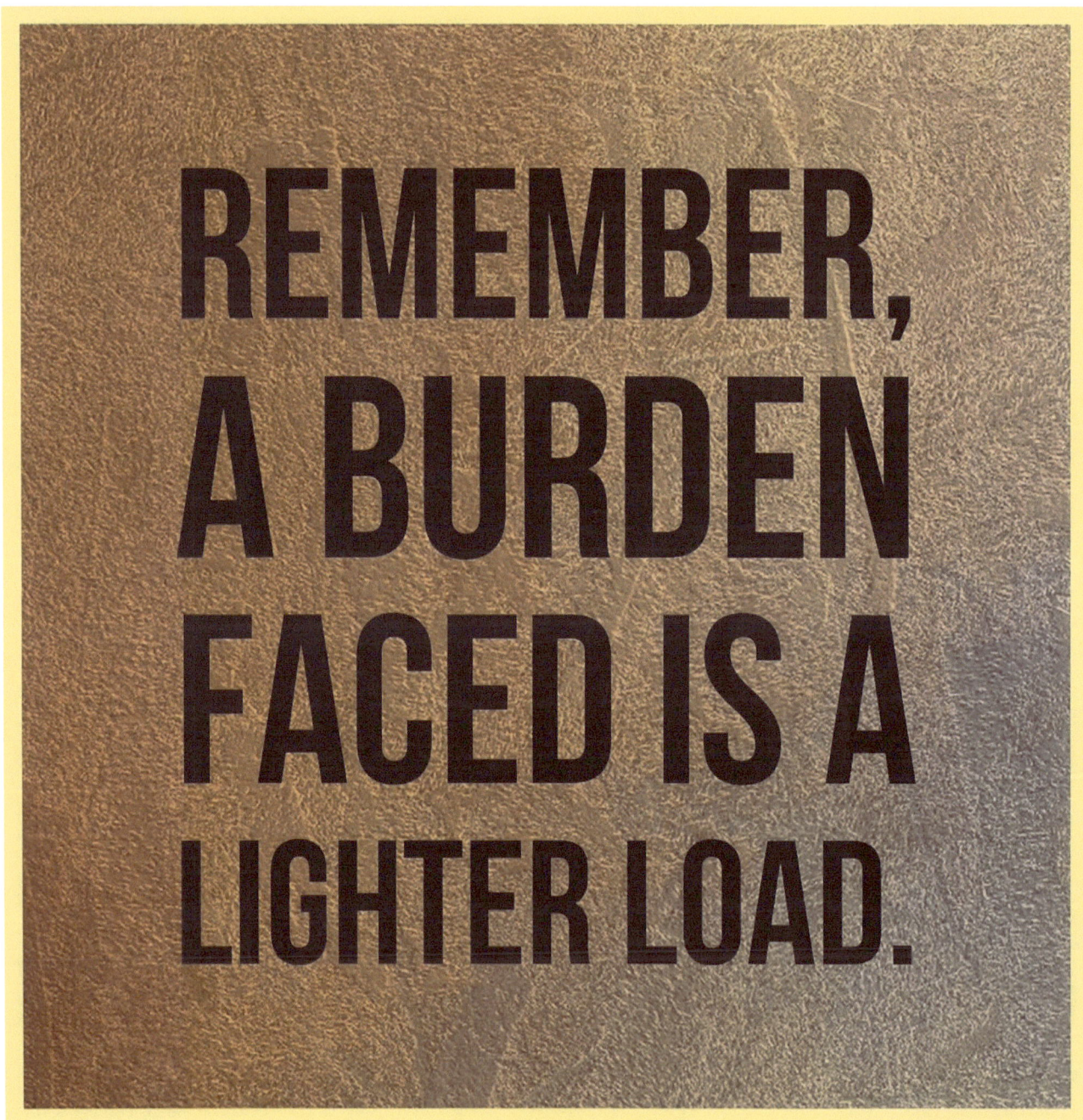

NO HEALTHY RELATIONSHIP IS A ONE-WAY STREET. BOTH **PARTIES MUST** FACE THE INEVITABILITY OF STRUGGLE. YOUR HORSE STRUGGLES JUST LIKE **YOU. A TRUE** EQUESTRIAN KNOWS THE SECRET PATH, THAT ONCE **TROUBLES ARE** ACCEPTED, THE HEART **WILL OPEN.**

A TRUE EQUESTRIAN HAS MORE TOOLS THAN PHYSICAL TECHNIQUES.

WHEN YOUR HORSE DOES SOMETHING AGAINST YOU, REMEMBER THAT FORGIVENESS IS AN ATTRIBUTE OF THE STRONG. THAT'S WHY WE ADMIRE THE HEART OF A HORSE BECAUSE THEY FORGIVE US OF OUR SHORTCOMINGS. BE MORE FORGIVING, **AND YOUR EQUESTRIAN SKILL WILL GROW.**

THE GREATEST TREASURES ARE HIDDEN IN THE DEEPEST PLACES.

TO CREATE A MORE EFFECTIVE RELATIONSHIP, REMEMBER TO THINK LIGHTLY OF YOURSELF AND DEEPLY ABOUT YOUR HORSE. CLOSENESS IN ANY RELATIONSHIP COMES FROM KNOWING THE SUBJECT OF YOUR AFFECTIONS.

THE DESIRE TO LEARN IS A THIRST FOR KNOWLEDGE.

WHEN YOUR HORSE IS ACTING UP, AND YOU FIND THE SADDLE UNCOMFORTABLE, KEEP THINGS SIMPLE. GO BACK TO THE BASICS; THINK OF YOURSELF AS A BEGINNER, THAT STATE OF MIND WILL MAKE ROOM FOR THE ANSWER.

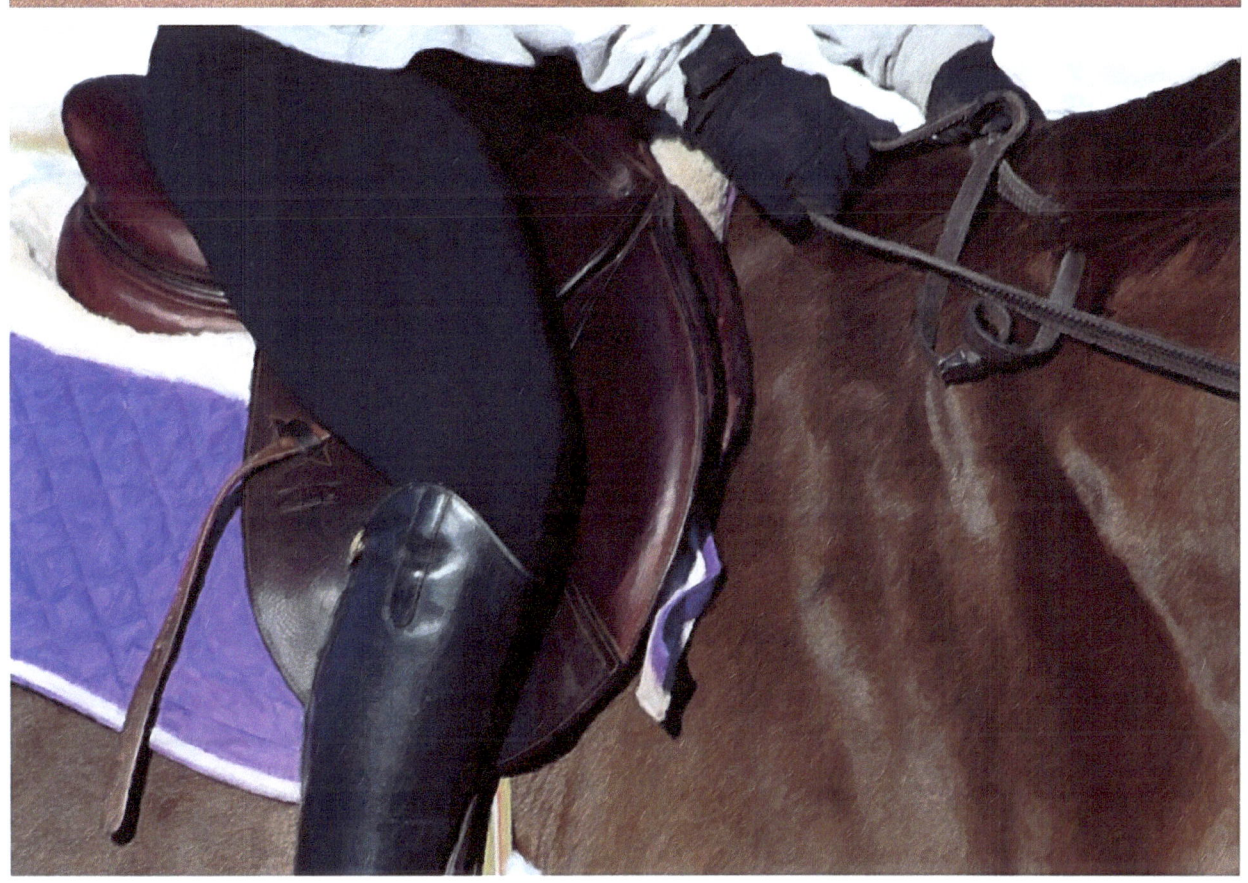

AWARENESS RAISES THE QUALITY OF AN EXPERIENCE.

ANYONE CAN SIT IN THE SADDLE AND GET CARRIED AROUND THE ARENA, THEN LATER TELL A STORY OF RIDING A HORSE. BUT TO SIT WITH AWARENESS, TO FEEL A BEATING, BREATHING, LIVING SOUL **UNDER YOUR SEAT IS TO EXPERIENCE** A HORSE. THAT IS THE ESSENCE OF RIDING, THE INTIMACY **OF AN EQUESTRIAN MOMENT.**

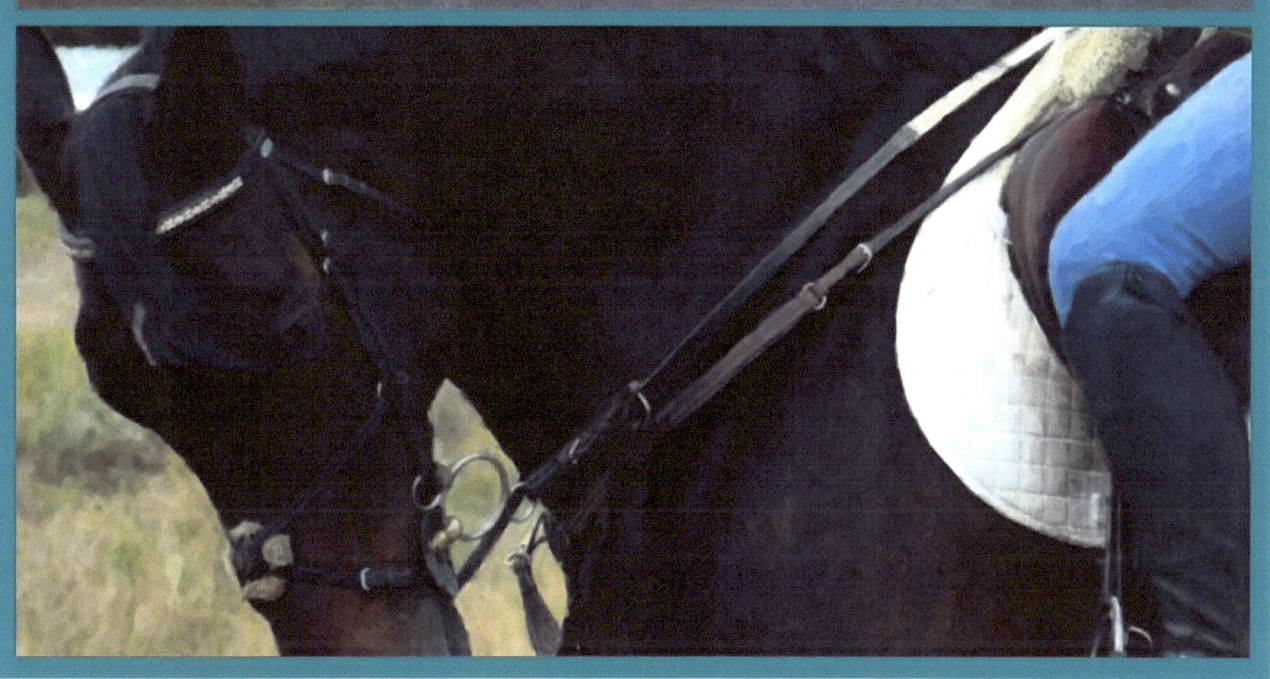

THERE IS MORE TO RIDING THAN LEARNING HOW TO RIDE.

TRUE EQUESTRIAN TECHNIQUE IS THE PRACTICE OF FORM TO GAIN AN EXPERIENCE THAT WILL BE USEFUL NOT ONLY IN THE ARENA, BUT ALSO IN LIFE.

THE SADDLE IS ONE OF THE MOST SIGNIFICANT SYMBOLS OF IRONY IN THE EQUESTRIAN WORLD. IT'S SHAPED INTO THE FORM OF A SEAT TO HOLD A **BODY; BUT REMEMBER, IT IS BEST TO HAVE AS FEW THOUGHTS AS POSSIBLE WHILE SITTING THERE.**

HAVE AS FEW THOUGHTS AS POSSIBLE

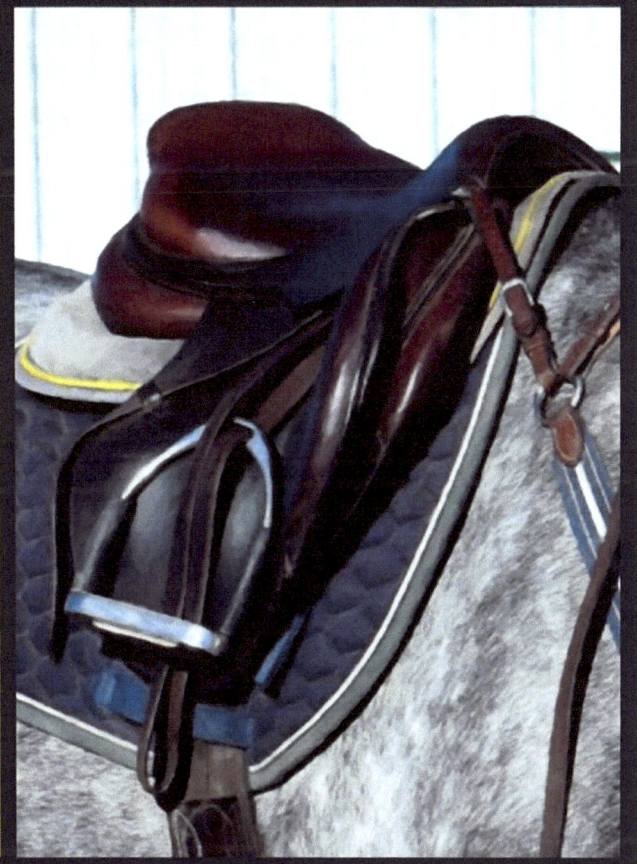

WHICH HORSE SHOWED UP TODAY? **THE SAINT, THE SINNER,** OR THE ROCK AND ROLLER? STAY FLEXIBLE, GO WITH **THE ENERGY** THAT PRESENTS ITSELF. RESISTANCE TO REALITY CREATES **OPPOSITION,** SURRENDER TO THE ENERGY OF THE MOMENT. IT HAS EVERYTHING YOU NEED.

STAY FLEXIBLE

EVERYTHING YOU NEED

TYPICALLY, WE ARE IN A STATE OF BARGAINING WITH OUR HORSE. PLEASE DO THIS, DON'T DO THAT. COOPERATE WITH ME NOW, AND I WILL FEED YOU LATER. LOVE IS A STATE OF FREEDOM, NOT A POSITION OF AUTHORITY.

EVALUATE THE CIRCUMSTANCES BEFORE TAKING ACTION.

STRIVE FOR UNDERSTANDING

WHEN YOUR HORSE IS UNCOOPERATIVE, SHE IS SENDING YOU A MESSAGE. TAKE CARE IN YOUR RESPONSE; PUNISHMENT MIGHT TEMPORARILY STOP THE BEHAVIOR BUT NOT FIND THE CURE. STRIVE FOR UNDERSTANDING; HORSEMANSHIP REQUIRES TOLERANCE; IT REQUIRES A COMPASSIONATE HEART.

SPONTANEITY CALLS FORTH ACTION FREE FROM COMPARISON.

WALK WITH YOUR HORSE WITHOUT ANY THOUGHT OF ARRIVING. THERE IS NO DESTINATION THAT CONTAINS WHAT YOU DESIRE. CLOSENESS IS FOUND IN THE MOMENT, INSIDE THE INTIMATE PRESENT.

GREAT IDEAS HAVE SYNERGY, NOT PURE AUTHORITY OVER EVERYTHING.

LETTING GO OF WHO YOU ARE

AN EQUESTRIAN RELATIONSHIP ISN'T ABOUT WORKING TOWARD SOME IDEAL. IT'S **ABOUT LETTING GO OF WHO YOU ARE, SURRENDERING TO A NEW DEFINITION OF** PARTNERSHIP. IDEAS DON'T SUPPORT COOPERATION; THEY SERVE IT.

DON'T BE AFRAID TO ATTEMPT SOMETHING NEW, SIT IN THE SADDLE IN A DIFFERENT WAY, GROOM YOUR HORSE WITH MORE TENDERNESS THAN BEFORE. WITHOUT A NOVEL EXPERIENCE, YOUR SENSE OF JUDGMENT WILL NEVER SHAPE YOUR PROGRESS.

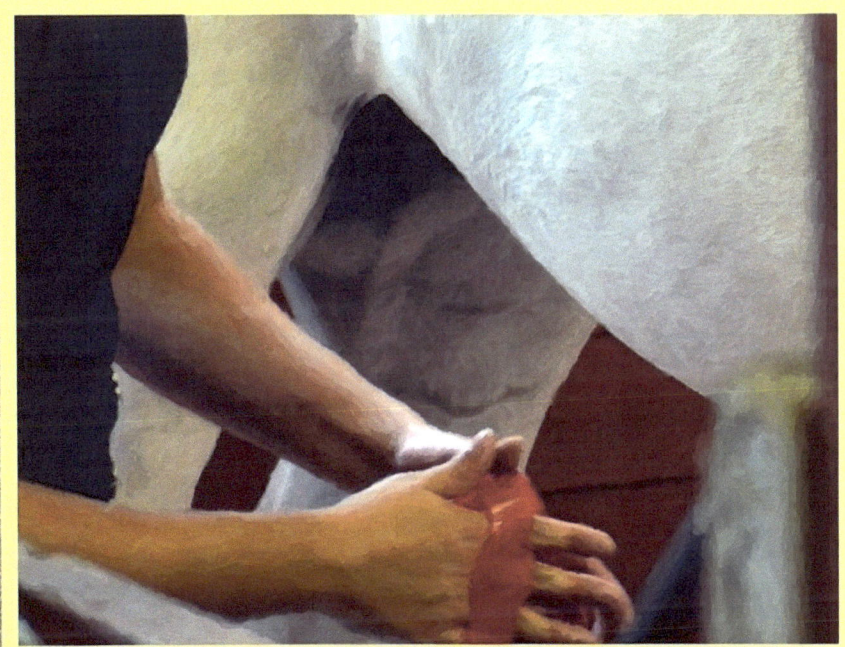

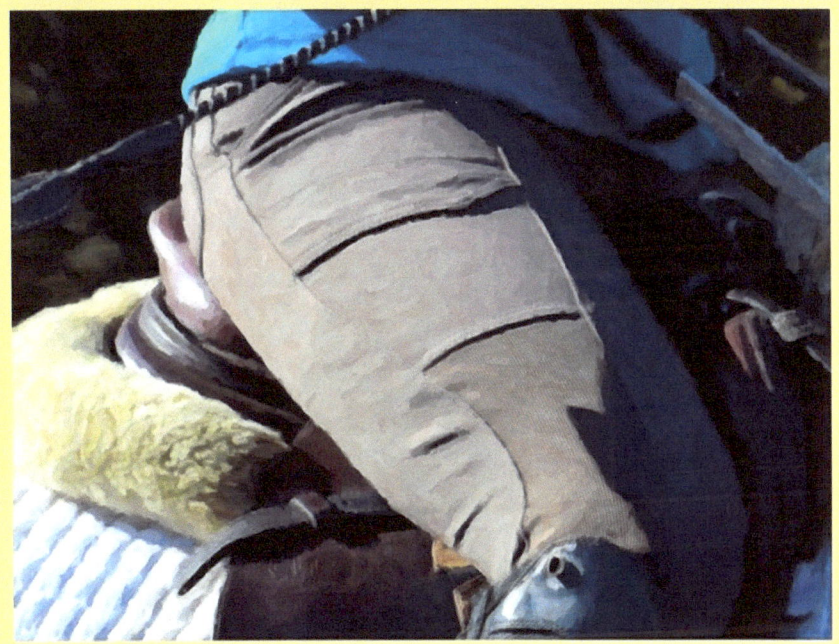

> **THERE IS MORE THAN ONE FORM OF INTELLIGENCE.**

BE A REBEL, GO AGAINST EVERYTHING YOU HAVE EVER BEEN TOLD ABOUT HORSEMANSHIP. TEST THE VERY DEPTHS OF THE ACCEPTED NORM, LET YOUR EXPERIENCE TELL YOU IF SOMETHING WORKS FOR YOU. USE YOUR INTELLIGENCE TO BUILD A UNIQUE RELATIONSHIP WITH YOUR HORSE, NOT SOMEONE ELSE'S IDEA OF CONNECTION.

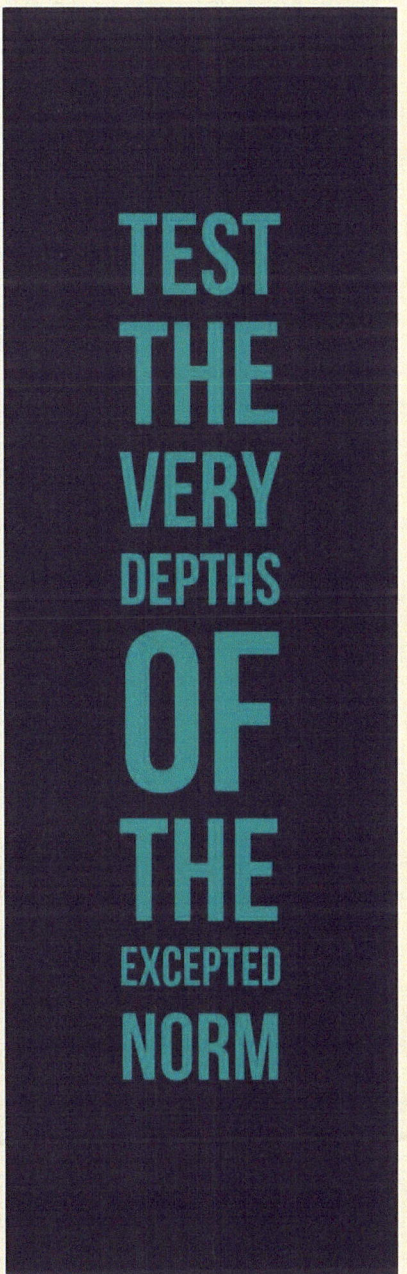

TEST THE VERY DEPTHS OF THE EXCEPTED NORM

LEARNING RARELY TAKES PLACE FROM A POSITION OF AUTHORITY.

VIEW THE RELATIONSHIP AS SOMETHING UNIQUE

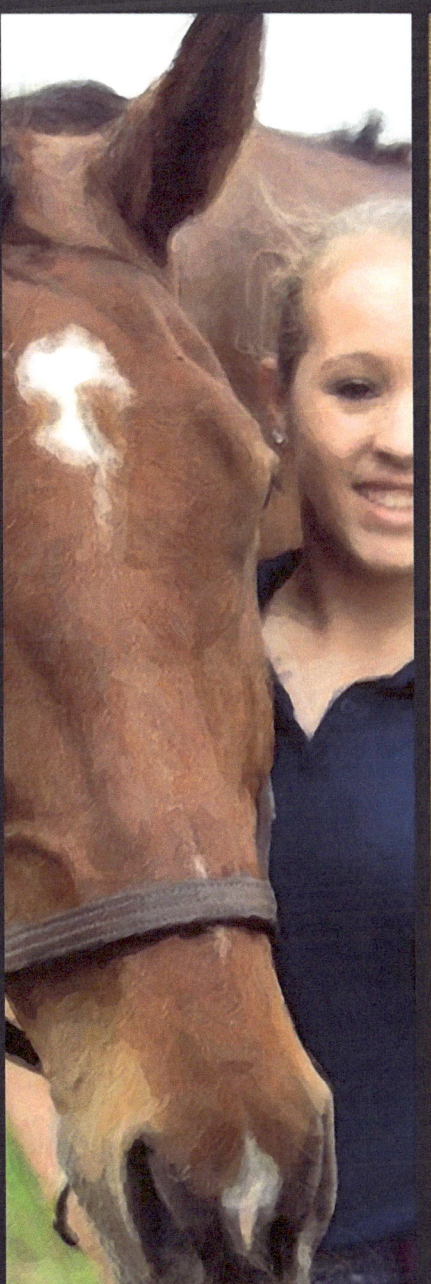

MEET YOUR HORSE ON EVEN GROUND, PUT YOURSELF IN A PLACE WHERE YOU ARE LEARNING SOMETHING FROM EXPERIENCE TOO. YOU ARE NOT SUPERIOR TO YOUR HORSE, NOR ARE YOU EQUAL. VIEW THE RELATIONSHIP AS SOMETHING UNIQUE. IT IS THE BEAUTY OF AN EQUESTRIAN MOMENT, THE INTIMACY BETWEEN FRIENDS.

IN ALL THINGS LOOK FOR WHAT IS REAL, THE LIVING PRESENCE.

TOUCH THE BEING OF A HORSE, REACH OUT WITH A NEW HAND. SEE THAT WHICH CANNOT BE SEEN BY OTHERS, EMBRACE THE ESSENCE OF THINGS. PERCEIVE THE LIVING, BEATING EQUESTRIAN HEART.

SEE THAT WHICH CANNOT BE SEEN

PERCEIVE THE LIVING

TAKE RESPONSIBILITY FOR THE QUALITY OF YOUR LIFE.

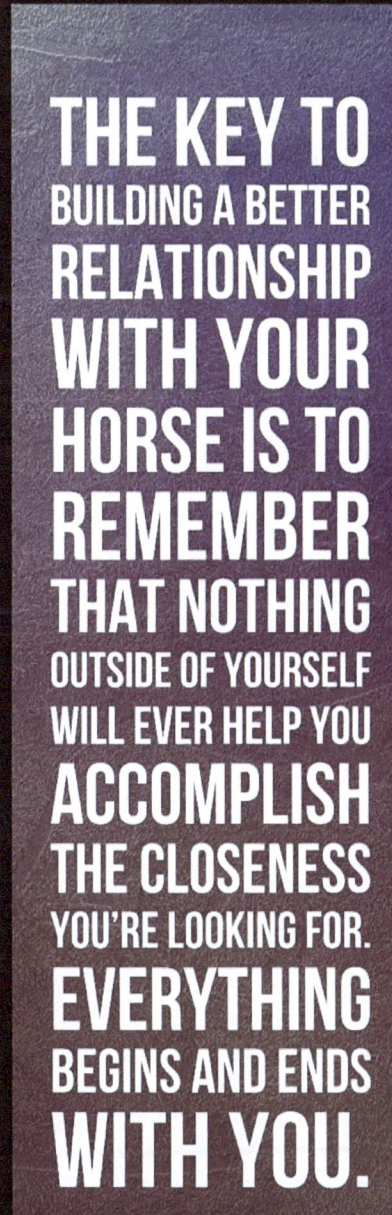

THE KEY TO BUILDING A BETTER RELATIONSHIP WITH YOUR HORSE IS TO REMEMBER THAT NOTHING OUTSIDE OF YOURSELF WILL EVER HELP YOU ACCOMPLISH THE CLOSENESS YOU'RE LOOKING FOR. EVERYTHING BEGINS AND ENDS WITH YOU.

THE CLOSENESS YOUR LOOKING FOR

THE LIFE OF A LIVING SOUL

THE HEART IS INSIDE THE BODY; IT BEATS WITH A BIOLOGICAL PULSE. BUT IT IS FAR MORE THAN AN ORGAN; IT IS THE LIFE OF A LIVING SOUL. PAY ATTENTION TO THE UNSEEN DETAILS, STRIVE TO UNDERSTAND THE ESSENCE OF A HORSE. DEVELOP A DISCERNMENT THAT BRINGS YOU CLOSER TO THE DEPTHS OF HORSE AND HUMAN RELATIONSHIPS.

REGRET TEACHES US HOW TO FORGIVE OURSELVES.

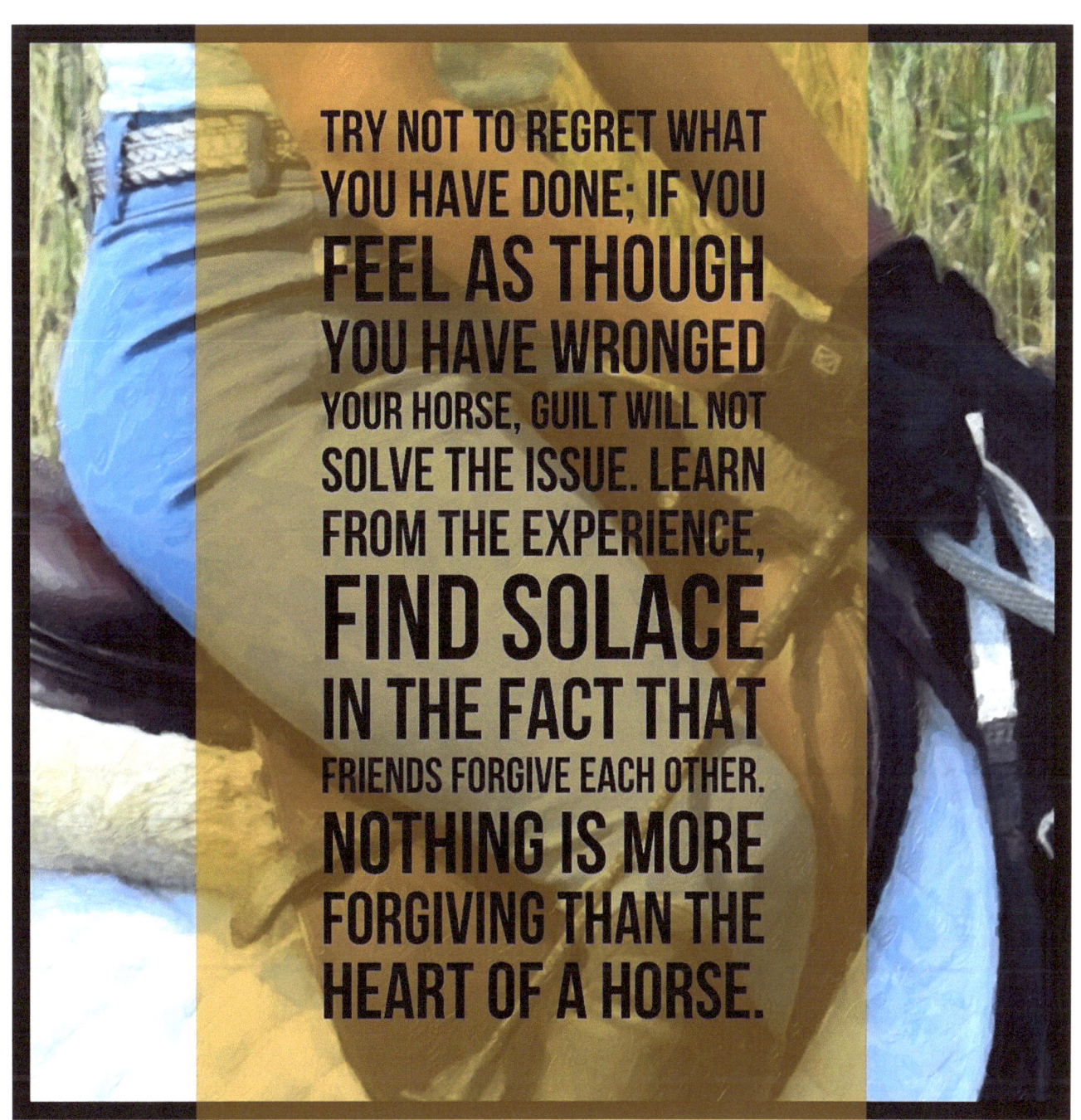

TRY NOT TO REGRET WHAT YOU HAVE DONE; IF YOU FEEL AS THOUGH YOU HAVE WRONGED YOUR HORSE, GUILT WILL NOT SOLVE THE ISSUE. LEARN FROM THE EXPERIENCE, FIND SOLACE IN THE FACT THAT FRIENDS FORGIVE EACH OTHER. NOTHING IS MORE FORGIVING THAN THE HEART OF A HORSE.

RISE ABOVE YOUR NEGATIVE STATES.

YOU HAVE INSIDE YOU ALL THE TENDERNESS, COMPASSION, AND EMPATHY TO FIND A CONNECTION TO YOUR HORSE. WHEN YOU LEARN TO **ACCEPT THAT BITTERNESS, GUILT, AND NEGATIVE** STATES DON'T MATTER, YOU WILL CROSS THE EQUESTRIAN BRIDGE BETWEEN HORSE AND HUMAN INTERACTION.

CROSS THE EQUESTRIAN BRIDGE

CULTIVATE ALL YOUR ABILITIES, INSIDE AND OUT.

YOU USE YOUR EYES TO SEE THE WORLD, BUT **YOU USE YOUR PERCEPTION** TO SEE THE HEART. IN EVERYTHING **EQUESTRIAN, USE YOUR** INNER ABILITIES TO GAIN A KNOWLEDGE **OF WHAT MATTERS,** NOT YOUR PHYSICAL SENSES.

GAIN A KNOWLEDGE
OF WHAT MATTERS

BALANCE YOURSELF IN THE SADDLE, PHYSICALLY AND EMOTIONALLY.

HAVE PATIENCE WHEN DEALING WITH YOUR HORSE, DON'T LET ITS BAD BEHAVIOR STEAL YOUR PEACE IN THE SADDLE. UNBALANCED EMOTIONS CREATE STRUGGLE, NOT COOPERATION.

FREEDOM CREATES UNRESTRICTED SPACE FOR COMMUNICATION TO FLOW.

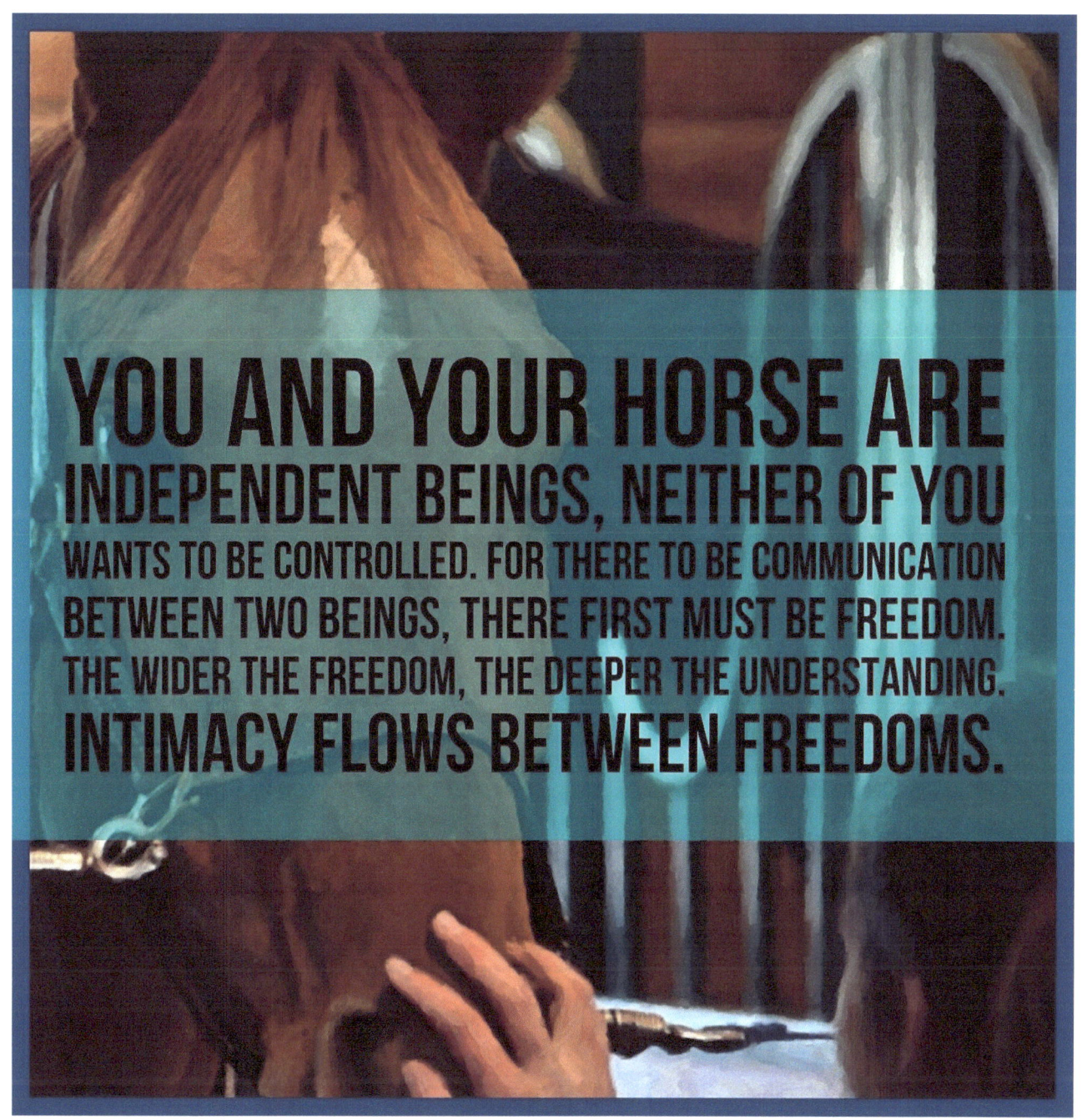

THE HEART REACHES OUT WHEN THE MIND IS QUITE.

WHEN YOU ARE FREE OF IDEAS, A MOMENT OF INTIMACY REVEALS ITSELF, AND YOU TOUCH THE HEART OF A HORSE.

TOUCH THE HEART OF A HORSE

LET YOUR MIND AND HEART WORK TOGETHER.

WHEN THE TIME IS RIGHT, BRING TOGETHER ALL THE PARTS TO FORM A WHOLE.

TO KNOW YOUR HORSE AS DEEPLY AS **POSSIBLE,** WHAT YOU DON'T NEED IS MORE INFORMATION, MORE COBWEBS IN THE MIND. WHAT YOU NEED IS THE ABILITY TO PERCEIVE HOW TO APPLY **WHAT YOU** ALREADY KNOW, **AND WHEN** TO USE IT. SO WHEN THE MOMENT PRESENTS **ITSELF, YOU CAN ACT WITH** PRECISION, NOT A GUESS **IN THE DARK.**

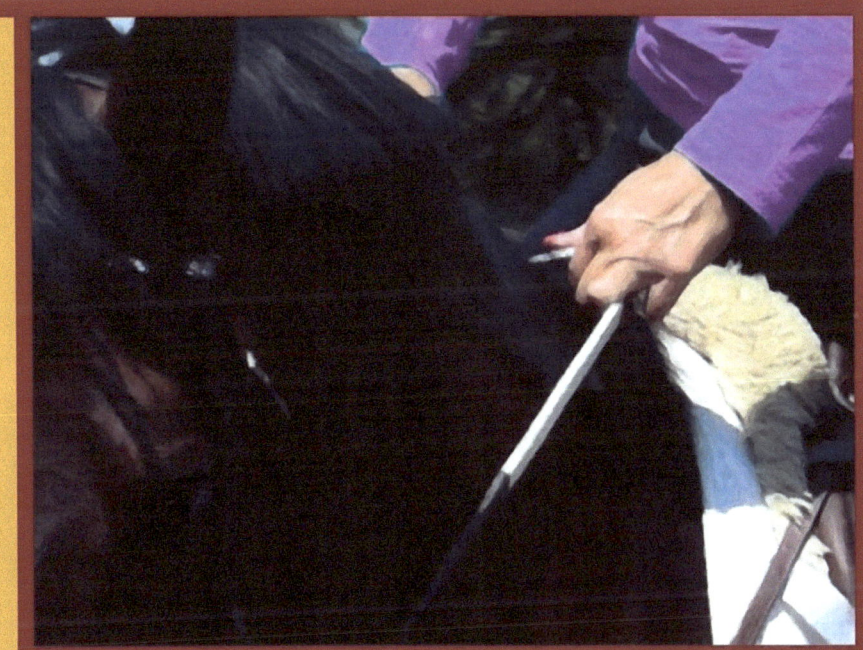

YOU CAN ACT WITH PRECISION

WHO OR WHAT DO YOU PUT YOUR TRUST IN?

QUIET YOUR MIND TO MAKE ROOM FOR TRUST TO ENTER.

TRUST EXISTS WHEN THERE IS OPENNESS

IF THERE IS A LACK OF TRUST BETWEEN YOU AND YOUR HORSE, FEAR COULD BE IN THE WAY. IS THERE SOMETHING BLOCKING EACH NOW FROM HAPPENING? CONFIDENCE EXISTS WHEN THERE IS AN OPENNESS TO THE MOMENT; IF THERE IS NOTHING THERE, THEN TRUST WILL ENTER.

THERE IS SOMETHING ELSE THERE

AWARENESS IS AN EXPANSIVE STATE, USE IT TO GAIN INFORMATION ESSENTIAL TO YOUR GOALS.

DON'T GET STUCK IN YOUR OWN THOUGHTS, BE FLEXIBLE ENOUGH TO LET THINGS HAPPEN.

FROM ONE THING TO ANOTHER

JUST MOVE ON

IF YOU'RE STRUGGLING WITH YOUR HORSE AND YOU DON'T KNOW WHY. DON'T SPEND TOO MUCH TIME TRYING TO FIGURE IT OUT. JUST MOVE ON, LIFE IS A FLOWING MOTION FROM ONE THING TO ANOTHER. KEEP MOVING; THEN THE ANSWER WILL COME.

LISTEN TO THE CREATIVE VOICE INSIDE; IT'S TRYING TO TELL YOU SOMETHING.

BE CREATIVE, TAKE CHANCES AND FIND WHAT WORKS **FOR YOU. EVERY** HORSE IS UNIQUE; EACH ONE HAS DIFFERENT NEEDS AND DESIRES. THERE IS NO ONE EQUESTRIAN **PHILOSOPHY** THAT WORKS FOR EVERYONE. FIND OUT WHAT BRINGS YOU RESULTS, **FOLLOW THE** JOY, LET THAT BE YOUR WAY.

LET JOY BE THE REASON FOR ALL YOUR RELATIONSHIPS.

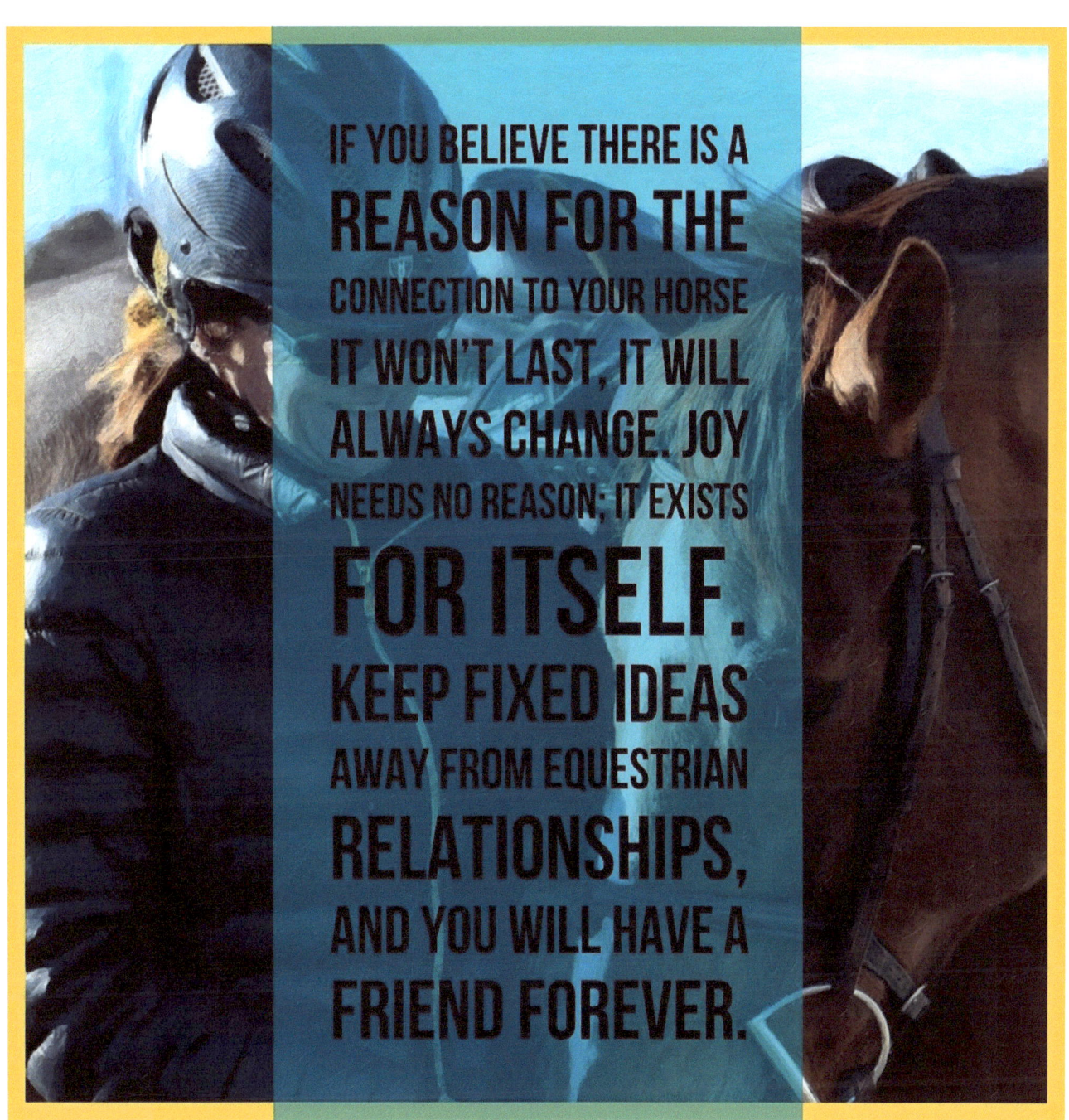

IF YOU BELIEVE THERE IS A **REASON FOR THE** CONNECTION TO YOUR HORSE IT WON'T LAST, IT WILL ALWAYS CHANGE. JOY NEEDS NO REASON; IT EXISTS **FOR ITSELF.** KEEP FIXED IDEAS AWAY FROM EQUESTRIAN **RELATIONSHIPS,** AND YOU WILL HAVE A FRIEND FOREVER.

IN THE END, YOU CAN'T CHANGE YOUR HORSE; YOU CAN ONLY CHANGE YOURSELF. IRONICALLY, CHANGING YOURSELF **BRINGS YOU CLOSER TO THE** EQUESTRIAN HEART, CHANGING YOUR HORSE.

YOU CAN ONLY CHANGE YOURSELF

BRINGS YOU CLOSER TO THE EQUESTRIAN HEART

KEEP YOUR FEET FIRMLY PLANTED IN THE STIRRUPS.

THE PERFECT HORSE IS THE ONE WHO WILL NEVER LET YOU DOWN, NEVER MISS A STRIDE, OR NEVER BREAK YOUR HEART. LEARNING IS BASED IN REALITY, THE EXISTENCE OF NOW. STOP DREAMING; TIME TO GO TO SCHOOL.

A FOCUSED RIDER MAKES A FOCUSED HORSE.

A HORSE IS AWARE OF THE SMALLEST CHANGE IN ENERGY; IT HAS AN INNATE CONNECTION TO ITS ENVIRONMENT. IT KNOWS YOU BETTER THAN YOU KNOW YOURSELF. WHEN YOU FEEL RUSHED IT MOVES QUICKER, IF YOU HESITATE, IT CHANGES DIRECTION. TO COMMUNICATE THE CORRECT **MESSAGE, STAY QUIET IN THE SADDLE.**

BRING FOCUS TO YOUR SENSES TO BRING YOU CLOSER TO THE MOMENT.

Absorb yourself in the **details of horsemanship**, see the color of each hair in the **mane**, feel the warmth of breath from the nose, the touch of a muzzle **that brings awareness.** There is closeness in those things, an **intimacy** of the moment that fosters relationship.

STRIVE TO APPRECIATE THE SUBTLE DETAILS, QUITE OFTEN THEY BRING THE MOST JOY.

IF YOU STRUGGLE WITH CLOSING THE GAP OF SEPARATION WITH YOUR HORSE; FOCUS ON THE SMALL THINGS. APPRECIATE THE SMALLEST DETAIL OF YOUR HORSE, THE **HEART IS GRAND,** BUT IT FITS INTO THE **TINIEST SPACES.**

ALIGN YOUR EXPECTATIONS WITH REALITY, AND THEY WILL SERVE YOU BETTER.

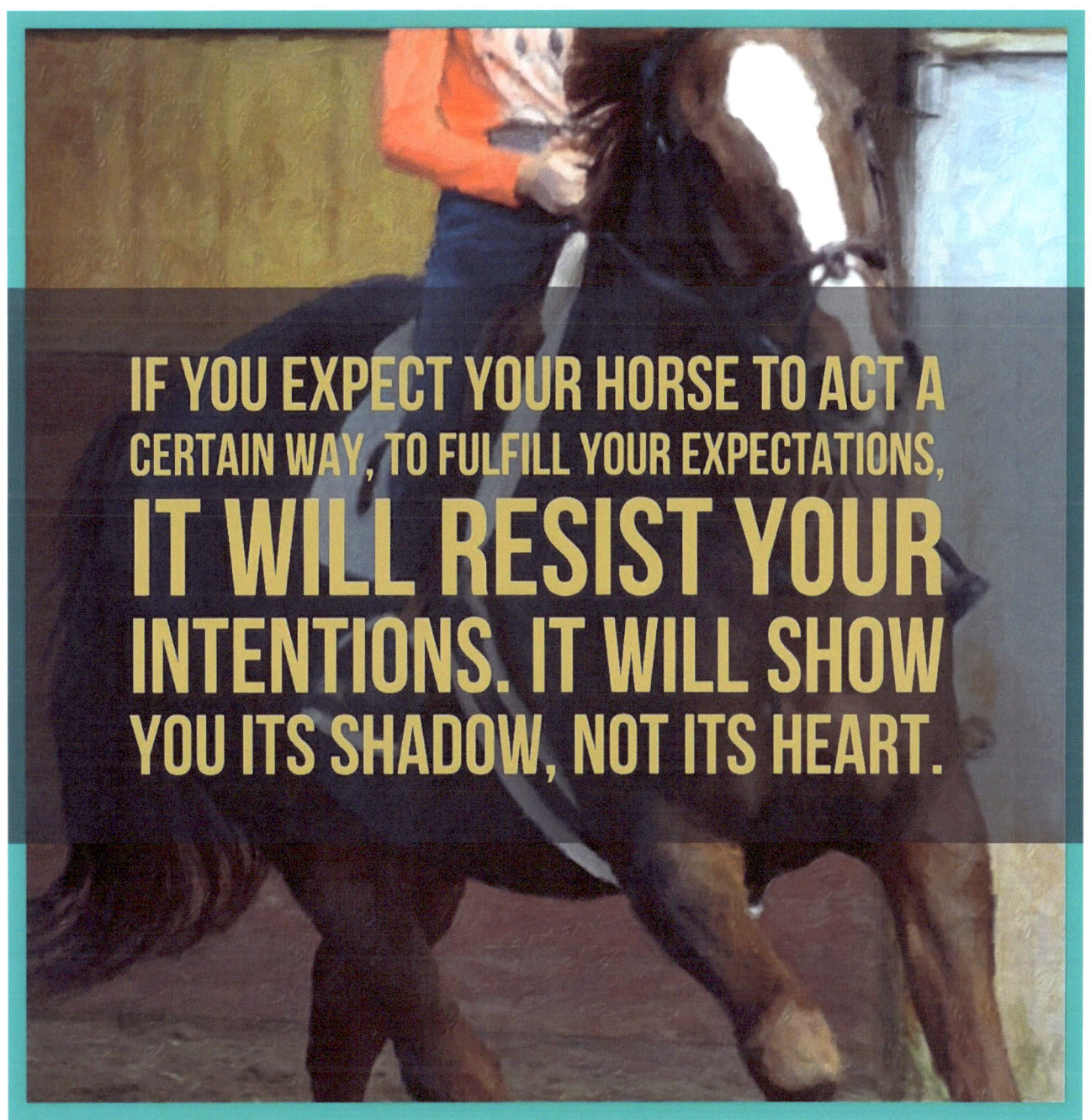

IF YOU EXPECT YOUR HORSE TO ACT A CERTAIN WAY, TO FULFILL YOUR EXPECTATIONS, IT WILL RESIST YOUR INTENTIONS. IT WILL SHOW YOU ITS SHADOW, NOT ITS HEART.

SOLITUDE AND JOY WALK HAND IN HAND.

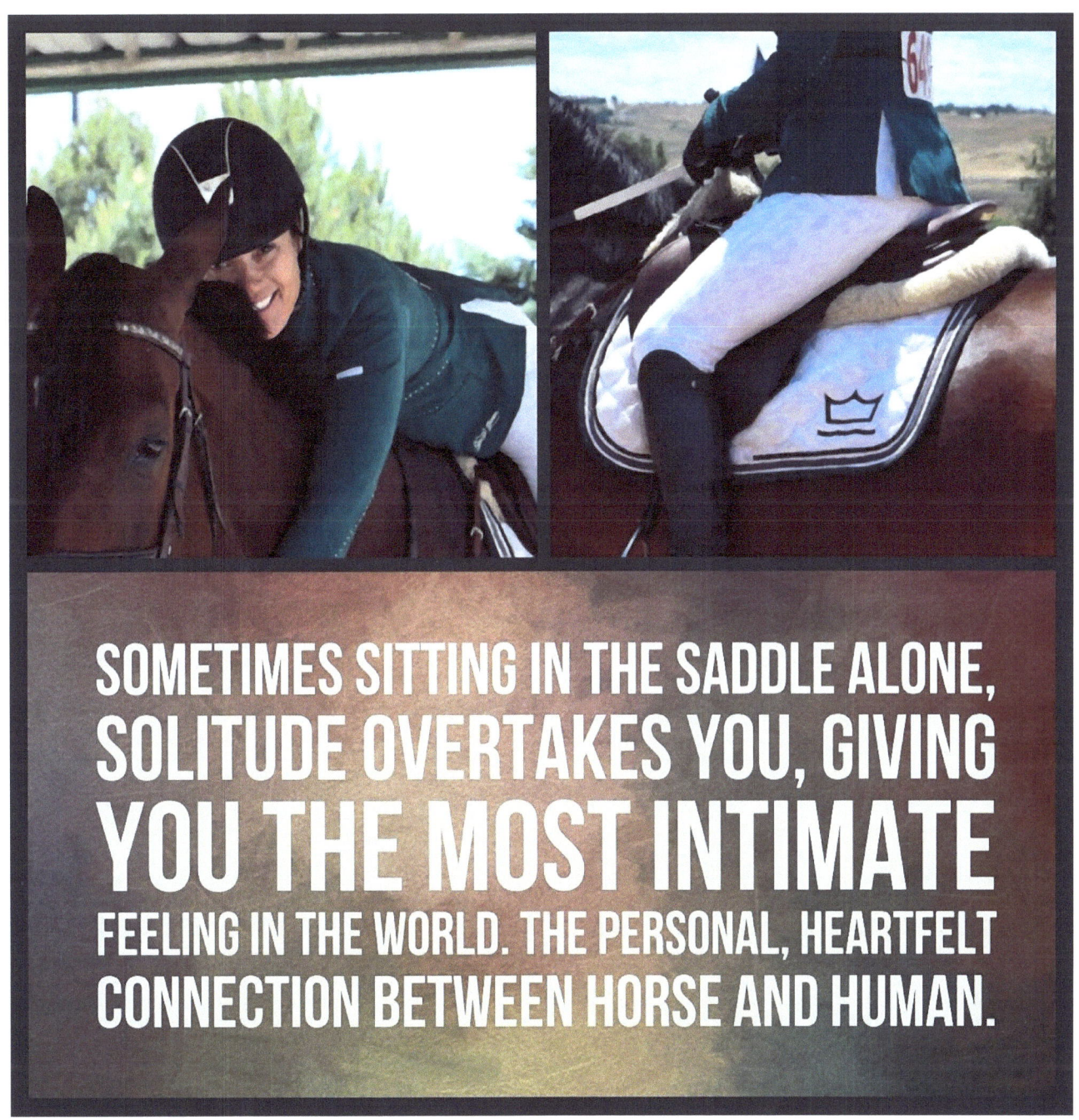

Marc Ness was born in Billings, Montana, and received his education from Montana State University, where he earned a bachelor's degree of science in psychology. He has a personal interest in mysticism and relationships. He has an affinity for horses and enjoys the outdoors. He lives and works in Denver, Colorado.